Positive Vibration:
Difficult Tin

Nicholas A Robertson

"At one time or the other in your life, you will feel forgotten by God. Yes, I said, *feel forgotten;* but the truth is that, even though that is how we feel sometimes, we know that God has never and will never leave us."

Edited by Petrena V Ledgister & Alexis O Ledgister

Book author for conferences, workshops, crusades, conventions, seminars, youth ministry, mentorship, men's ministry and couple's ministry.

Email: reasonwithrobdon@gmail.com

Website: reasowithrobdon.com

Follow us: Reason with Robdon

Published by: Reason with Robdon

Book Cover Design by: Iconic Presence

ISBN: 978-1-7773659-1-2

PREFACE

In the words of Victor Hugo, "Nothing is more powerful than an idea whose time has come." This statement aptly describes this book by my brother, friend and fellow minister Nicholas "Robdon" Robertson as he makes his entrance on the stage of authorship. I believe that this book is significant, relevant and applicable, especially in view of the many and varied challenges being faced at this time. People are looking for answers, not theories. "Positive Vibration: Navigating Through Difficult Times", was borne out of the seed of a thought that mushroomed into this most significant roadmap, purposed with helping countless individuals face the rigors of life with a plan that is solution driven.

This is not some pie-in-the-sky work, but a practical and systematic real-life version of the various types of ordeals that humans face and how, with the help of principles undergirded by scriptures, they can face their reality. This current volume is a derivative of his daily online programme Positive Vibrations and seeks to expose all and sundry to the tools of critical thinking that are important in examining and addressing your reality from God's perspective.

You cannot read this volume and not see his heart. A heart filled with a desire to be a skilled helper in providing the tools and directions needed to traverse this terrain of life. Nicholas exposes himself in this book as a teacher, friend, confidant, encourager, and servant who is most willing to accompany you on this journey as partner and guide. The pages come alive with both precepts and examples and are written with such clarity that provides ease of understanding and application readiness.

His skilful use of stories to highlight principles makes this work adaptable to the uniqueness of our individual situations. The imageries are powerful and emphasise such themes as trust, relationship, love, obedience, the wilderness, and sacrifice, making this book an invaluable tool for everyday living and a must for your individual library and upkeep. Nicholas takes us on a unique journey that is life- transforming and challenges us to confront our circumstances as he reminds us that God will sustain us during the times of hardships, but we have to submit to his will and authority in our lives.

As we read this book, it is evident that the purpose is not solely for information but transformation. This book will serve as a useful guide as we navigate the difficult times. Don't struggle with the lessons, just learn from the experiences; it will provide invaluable insights which are applicable in a myriad of real-life situations. This is a great tool for individual study, small groups, the churched and unchurched communities based on its relevance. It's valued for its contribution whether you have been through, are currently facing or are preparing for a challenging time.

The effective use of scriptures gives us a Divine assurance that we have the right pilot in charge, one who is experienced in all the challenges of life and is committed to our overall welfare.

Get ready for the journey of a lifetime and pay keen attention to all the signals and instructions as you remain positive, navigating through difficult times.

Tough times don't last, tough people do (Robert Schuller).

Rev. Valentine Rodney

Author, Director – Word Impact Ministries International

ABOUT THE AUTHOR

NICHOLAS A. ROBERTSON, Dip.Min (Hon.), Dip.Ed (Hon.), BD (Hon.) B. Ed (Hon.) M.Ed (Hon.) is a dynamic speaker, counselor, mentor and educator who meticulously uses his expertise from military service and his pedagogy to expound on the principles of the Kingdom of God. From as early as 2006, he has been actively involved in ministry and his service transcends borders. To date, he has served in Jamaica, the United States and the United Kingdom. Rev Robertson has operated in the following areas: Youth Ministry, Evangelism, Christian Education, Leadership, Radio and Social Media ministry.

He studied at the Church Teacher's College, University of the West Indies, Mona, United Theological College of the West Indies and the Christian Leaders College.

He is the founder of Positive Vibration, a daily devotional on social media; cohost of Mr. & Mrs. Robdon's Couples Corner and is also the founder and COO of BuildAMan Foundation, a non-profit initiative to develop Godly men, husbands and fathers.

Living in the digital age, he remains resolute that strategic evangelism, intentional discipleship, relationship, and technology must play an active role in reaching people with the gospel of Jesus Christ. He strongly advocates that the Word of God, when taught, is for rebuke, reproof and exhortation. Being cognizant of this, the believer must create an action plan to undergo application in order to experience transformation.

He is married to Danielle and the union has produced two children, Danick and Danice.

ENDORSEMENTS

'Positive Vibration: Navigating Through Difficult Times', authored by Nicholas Robertson, is not just a book filled with stories and Bible verses. It is a book with true experiences that have been shared from a heart of love. When you turn its pages and read the author's life experiences, I am sure that you can all identify with its contents; it is easy for us to get discouraged and throw in the towel. It is also easy for us to listen to the lies of the devil, instead of lifting our faith. At one time or the other in your life, you will feel forgotten by God. Yes, I said, *feel forgotten;* but the truth is that, even though that is how we feel sometimes, we know that God has never and will never leave us. In retrospect, this book is a reminder of God's constant presence with us as we go through our depressing, and often, unwanted situations.

From cover to cover, the writer desires that you be encouraged as you read through its pages. He has carefully chosen the topics with you in mind and they are relevant to any time and season. The words of encouragement are not limited to race, colour or creed. They are not limited by landmarks but apply to all those who love the Lord and are for those who wish to have an intimate relationship with him. If you know Nicholas Robertson well, I am sure that you will agree that he practises what he preaches. He has also adopted the saying from Dr. Myles Munroe,

“The word of God is not just for information, but for transformation.” I trust that as you read this book, your life will change for the better.

Mrs Petrena V Ledgister
Editor Translator & Educator of Spanish- UK

In the book, "Positive Vibration: Navigating Through Difficult Times (Volume 1)." Nicholas Robertson has created a work that is rich in biblical and Christian principles. He is theologically insightful and direct to share with all, especially those who struggle to overcome personal hardships. The depth of the material throughout the book, makes it ideal for personal devotions, reflections, and prayerful declarations. As a Christian Pastor, I can’t wait to share this gift with those I am called to serve*!*

Leo C. Hall
Pastor, Author, Conference Speaker

Nicholas Robertson is a young man full of passion for Jesus and a firm believer in constantly giving off positive vibrations.

These vibrations are contagious. He has brought that same excitement, enthusiasm and passion to the pages of his first book “Positive Vibration: Navigating Through Difficult Times.”

This is a well written volume which is quite fitting for this season. It guides the reader through various words of abundant promises from the scriptures that will help one to navigate through difficulties and propel them to experience God's peace.

This book will get your undivided attention from the first page. Happy reading.

Evangelist Jean Fullerton

TABLE OF CONTENTS

DEDICATION

Beverley Sills opines, "There are no shortcuts to any place worth going." Certainly, the completion of this milestone is another step along the journey of fulfilment. The reality of this vision is hinged on the contribution of some destiny helpers. I would therefore like to dedicate this book to the following:

- Firstly, to my awesome wife, Danielle Brown Robertson. Hon, as expected, you stood with me and aided my advancement while navigating one of the most difficult junctures of our life. You prayed, advised, encouraged, supported and most importantly tolerated. I love you.

- Secondly, to my wonderful children, Danick and Danice. We turned your home into a daily church, forcing you to adapt. Though young, you guys made some great partners in a difficult season. Dad deeply appreciates you.

- Thirdly, to my Positive Vibration Team. We have prayed, worshipped, and studied the word of God together. You have been faithful in supporting this vision and for that I want to express sincere gratitude.

- Finally, to the ministers, workers, prayer team, worship team, technical team and those who offered ongoing support through encouragement and testimonies. You have demonstrated the true effect of collaboration, support, and teamwork.

ACKNOWLEDGEMENT

Writing a book is not something one does every day. In fact, "Positive Vibrations, navigating through Difficult Times," is my first book and it has been quite a rewarding journey. Since it is God that has given me the talent and ability to write, I would like to thank Him first and foremost. Without His leading, wisdom, strength and help, this book would only be still a thought.

Secondly, I would like to thank my dear wife Danielle, who has been my support. Whenever I have a project to do, I can always be sure that she will be there for me. She gave me some amount of inspiration and has kept the children occupied or out of my way when I needed the time to write.

Thirdly, a big thank you to my brother in Christ and friend, Reverend Valentine Rodney, who has been one of my constant coaches and cheerleaders. Along the way, he has been a reliable listening ear and a trusted adviser. Thank you very much.

Fourthly, I would like to express thanks to Petrena and Alexis Ledgister who have edited this book. Theirs has been an immense help and I am grateful. Petrena, thanks for encouraging me to use the stories and testimonies as the backbone for the book. I know that many people can relate to them.

I would also like to say a big thank you to Oneil Brown from Iconic Presence for designing the book cover. It is attractive and, one can truly judge this book by its cover.

To those who have read the book and whose endorsements are published therein, Reverend Leo Hall, Evangelist Jean Fullerton, and Dr Pepe Ramnath (by way of the foreword), I owe you a debt of gratitude.

To others who have read, endorsed, and prayed for the completion of the book, I thank the Lord for you, and I thank you too.

FOREWORD

If you are a student of the message of Jesus, the kingdom of Heaven, then you have picked up the right book. This young leader and author, Nicholas 'Robdon' Robertson, has compressed and expressed his personal experiences to enlighten and teach us how to navigate through difficult times in this timely series locked in Volume one.

This book has heavenly instructions that are certainly endowed with power to teach us how to remain optimistic in a globally challenging world. It was carefully written with you in mind to keep your head up in these adverse times of testing. Your system of thinking is about to be challenged as you begin your journey into this amazing revelation. You are now invited to unlock the mysteries and nuggets of this volume and use these instructions to successfully conquer this season of your life.

Robdon's approach to the subject of navigation was carefully crafted and written for readers looking for an introductory, intermediate, and advanced study of the kingdom dominion. The progression into the heart of Jesus' message is felt in each chapter, which brings a new level of freedom and motivation for life. These chapters will take you further into the chambers of the kingdom that you have never seen or experienced before as you 'vibrate and settle positively' amidst chaos and confusion.

The author shows us that there are no shortcuts to victory and success. He used the life of the Apostle Paul who is no stranger to challenges and roadblocks in the equation of life. Robdon shared in his own words, "Deliverance from a situation is not always an extracted elevation out of, or an instant end to, oppression." He went on to further state, "Sometimes God wants to promote endurance and showcase His ability to sustain in hardships. Paul, an apostle of the Lord, credited for writing approximately fourteen of the twenty-seven books of the New Testament, was afflicted with an uncomfortable thorn in the flesh. He prayed three times for deliverance but was still unable to persuade God to alter His divine will. We are instruments created for God's glory; thus, He reserves the right to make the final ruling."

The question was asked as to how many times do we sink into depression because our problems fail to be resolved immediately. He encourages us to focus on our purpose rather than the issues we face. Calibrating our focus is truly the intention of Mr. Robertson. It was especially encouraging to me when he cited the lives of Paul and Silas in prison, "It was in prison that Paul and Silas offered up prayers that erupted into worship and invited the presence of God which shook the stronghold open, and dismantled the shackles and the yokes of bondage."

This book will revive the original thoughts, ideas and intentions of Jesus to navigate through life's difficulties and to reassure us that our purpose is greater than our situations at hand. I remember one of Dr. Myles Munroe's sons, Hubert, telling me that Dr. Munroe would regularly say, "My purpose is greater than the turbulence" when he would be caught up in turbulence. This book will immediately eliminate any possible confusion and irony and propel you back into positive vibration.

There is hope in a new voice, yet an old philosophy. This philosophy has given us hope again and a new understanding in the content of this timely book. From the author's personal experiences to his military adventures, he clearly gives us the hope we desperately need in the fragile economic, social and political spheres of the society of today.

The Positive Vibration: Navigating Through Difficult Times (Volume 1) is a book which gives us our true measure and reminds us of the model for repairing our broken histories to conquer and navigate through difficult times. We can find the life we need to live again amidst change. This book was written for the destruction of our ignorance and for us to enjoy life while facing challenges.

May we glean, from the writing of this book, the wisdom that shines from each page unto the pathways of our destiny. May the symphony of our King's grace increase over our lives every time we pick up this script.

We are more than conquerors with positive vibration in this journey of life.

R. Pepe Ramnath, PhD

EO-UN Ambassador/Scientist

Miramar Kingdom Community Center, Florida, USA

Chapter 1

Relationship Wins Every Time

Christ has truly set us free. Now make sure that you stay free, and don't get tied up again in slavery to the law. (Galatians 5: 1 NLT)

Some years ago, my pastor shared a story with me about a young lady named Kerry who was pulled over on the highway for speeding in a 60-kilometer speed zone. In addition, the officer booked her for intoxication as a close examination of the vehicle revealed she was drinking. The following day she was summoned to court to be tried. On realizing that the judge presiding over her case was her very own father she became extremely hopeful of a favourable verdict. She whispered to the officer escorting her, "The judge is my dad" boastfully.

When faced with trouble, talk big: I am guilty BUT now "there is no condemnation for those who belong to Christ Jesus." (Romans 8:1 NLT)

Pray with me: "*Lord I am confident that whereas the charge was guilty, you are not condemning me*".

I want to declare that guilt is not a synonym for condemnation. You are guilty but not condemned.

The offence committed by Kerry was punishable by law and she could receive up to one (1) year in prison or be fined a total of one million dollars Jamaican dollars.

Similarly, sin was punishable by death.

Declare with me: "Death and destruction will not be my portion. Deliverance cometh!"

The prosecutor presented a convincing case to the judge. However, despite having a compelling argument against her, Kerry was emphatically sure her father would pardon her.

Declare this: "When all odds are against me, my relationship with the father will determine the outcome. No matter how bad it gets, it will work out in my favour."

To her surprise, the judge banged the gavel against the bench and declared the words, "Guilty! Maximum fine or twelve (12) months in prison!" With her mouth wide open in disbelief, Kerry lamented, "How could my father be so wicked? He is supposed to love me. He knows I am not working and am unable to pay that kind of money. I am going to prison for a whole year."

Though an unfavourable verdict has been passed, remember the outcome will be determined by the relationship with the Father. What is your relationship with the great judge, Yahweh?

Pray with me: *"Lord, I submit as son/daughter to a father. I am yours and you are mine. Amen!"*

The officer proceeded to put on the handcuffs and whispered, "I guess your father had to do the right thing regardless of your relationship". What Kerry was learning in that moment was that her father, as judge, had a responsibility to interpret the law, analyze the evidence presented and make an impartial ruling on the matter. Regardless of the relationship they shared, her father was the judge and should act accordingly. Many times, as Christians we assume that because our father is loving and merciful and because we have asked for forgiveness, we should escape the consequences of our actions. Not only did the Lord invent humanity but he presented us a manual outlining his expectations and the consequences for transgressing the laws.

I want to declare that: Yahweh is the Just God! He will rule Right every time, even when those rules are not appealing. Your relationship with the father will determine the conclusion.

Let us pray: "*God I know you are perfect in all you do. You are immaculate at heart and impeccable in nature. Help me to accept those rulings that may bring me pain for a season. I want to renew my commitment to you as a son/daughter for my relationship will decide the outcome.*"

Today I have given you the choice between life and death, between blessings and curses. Now I call on heaven and earth to witness the choice you make. Oh, that you would choose life, so that you and your descendants might live! (Deuteronomy 30: 19NLT)

God invited the host of heaven and the inhabitants of the earthly realm to a dramatic court hearing to choose one from each package presented: life or death, blessing or curse, hoping that Israel would opt for life and blessing. He sought to persuade them to accept life by bringing awareness to the benefits promised to them and their offspring. God's word is perfect, and it determines the status of our relationship with Him. To transgress is to tell the Judge and Father, "I do not love you". A relationship is deemed good when there is mutual gain. The Judge knows your heart based on how well you submit to the laws.

"If you love me, obey my commandments. (St. John 14: 15 NLT)

Your extreme adherence to the laws is an indication of how you perceive Him in the relationship.

Pray with me: *"Lord help me observe and do all that is in your holy word. Help me to use it for planning, decision making and even for simple situations."*

There are consequences for transgressing the laws of God and therefore, as a people, we are called to order our steps based on the Word of God.

Your word is a lamp to guide my feet and a light for my path. (Psalm 119:105 NLT)

Declare with me: "My relationship will determine the outcome. There is a direct correlation between my submission to the Word of God and my love for Him."

"Officer! Officer!" A cry issued from the judge's chambers. "Sorry, I guess the judge is not done with you yet young lady. Let us go." the officer instructed.

Any violation of the laws gives room for the enemy's ridicule. Obedience determines the status of the relationship.

On entering the office, Kerry saw the judge, who was her father up to a couple hours ago before transforming into a fierce monster, moving his robe. She yelled, "Who are you? I cannot believe that you are really allowing me to go to prison."

"You are not going to prison" the judge responded. She answered, "What do you mean? Are you suffering from amnesia?"

The judge explained "Earlier today, I was your judge, and, in that capacity, I am expected to be just. You were guilty and the offence committed deserved one year in prison if you were unable to pay the fine. Now, I am your dad and I love you unconditionally. Despite your wrongdoing you are still my little girl and therefore I have paid the fine for you. As your dad I could not allow you to be incarcerated."

God in His infinite wisdom, who saw that we were guilty even before we committed the transgression, implemented a redemption plan. "For this is how God loved the world: He gave his one and only Son, so that everyone who believes in him will not perish but have eternal life." (St. John 3:16NLT)

Today, when we pray, we face God as the loving father who has paid the fine by sacrificing his own son so we will not have to be sent away to an eternal prison. We are guilty but are made right by faith because of God's undying love.

Therefore, since we have been made right in God's sight by faith, we have peace with God because of what Jesus Christ our Lord has done for us. (Romans 5: 1NLT)

As with the Galatians, we have been made free by God, therefore we are supposed to stand in this freedom. Sometimes the scars of yesterday may cause us to think we have to do something additional to be saved. However, such a view is erroneous: the price was completely paid on the cross. We do not need work out our own way to pay for the offence committed; God freed us from sin, guilt, condemnation, and the power and presence of sin.

So now there is no condemnation for those who belong to Christ Jesus. And because you belong to him, the power of the life-giving Spirit has freed you from the power of sin that leads to death. (Romans 8:1-2NLT) Much to Kerry's amazement, the officer walked down and relieved her from the cuffs and declared, "You are free to go". As with Kerry, the bonds and shackles of sin are released when we accept the gift of God-grace (the free unmerited and undeserved favour of God).

Relationship wins every time. The love of God supersedes any wrong you have indulged in.

Kerry hugged her dad and was about to rush out when her father called to her saying "I love you, please stay out of my courthouse. You are free; stay free!"

It is easy to be free but difficult to remain free. Paul charged the Galatians to remain free. This suggests that it takes an even greater effort to remain free. Kerry will now have to live the required standards of her city to not find herself in bondage again. Once we have been set free from sin, we have the responsibility to live by the instructions within the Holy Apostolic Writings.

Your laws are my treasure; they are my heart's delight (Psalm 119:111NLT)

Kerry had the privilege of living without guilt for her past error. It is easy to feel guilty over our past mistakes so much so that we condemn ourselves. We are sometimes our harshest judge, always trying our cases, and sanctioning guilty verdicts. Free yourselves from emotional and psychological bondage.

So, if the Son sets you free, you are truly free. (John 8: 36 NLT)

It is also possible to be free and live in bondage. Kerry had to recognize and accept she was free and then proceed to live in freedom. Many Christians, though they prayed for forgiveness years ago, continue to live with the pain of the yoke of sin. Release yourselves from prison.

Evangelist D. L Moody shared a story years ago about a former slave woman who lived in the South of America. After the Civil War, she received news that she had been freed. However, she was unsure, so she asked her peers and they said, "Yes you are free, President Abraham Lincoln signed a new proclamation supporting our freedom".

Jesus our great King of kings has signed the greatest proclamation declaring your freedom.

"If you openly declare that Jesus is Lord and believe in your heart that God raised him from the dead, you will be saved." (Romans 10:9 NLT)

Still in doubt, the one-time slave went to confirm the accuracy of the information with her former master who told her, "You are not free: no such proclamation was signed." She was confused, not knowing who to believe. Similarly, many of you have continued to listen to the residual lies of the old man, the world, and the devil.

Lift your hands and declare with me: "I am who God says I am; I am free from my sins. I am now released from custody in Jesus' name."

But now you are free from the power of sin and have become slaves of God. Now you do those things that lead to holiness and result in eternal life (Romans 6:22 NLT)

Now that you are free, walk in the Spirit. It is only by walking in the Spirit that we can escape our sinful nature.

"I say, let the Holy Spirit guide your lives. Then you won't be doing what your sinful nature craves." (Galatians 5:16 NLT)

Notice what the judge told Kerry in his closing remarks. "I love you, please stay out of my courthouse. You are free; stay free. Kerry may need to obtain a driving manual and to enroll in a driving course where she will have an instructor to help her maneuver to mitigate her erring again in similar fashion. We too must study the Word of God and surrender to our driving instructor the Holy Spirit. The Holy Spirit resides in us as our teacher, advisor, and mediator to provide support that prevents us from falling prey to the old adamic nature, the world and the devil. We are to adhere to the influence of the Holy Spirit.

And I will ask the Father, and he will give you another Advocate, who will never leave you. (St John 14:16)

Jesus in His exit speech assured the disciples that He would plead with His father to send <u>another</u> comforter. The word 'another' in ancient Greek is 'allen' which meant "another of the same kind". As with the disciples, we are assured that we have access to similar help as that which Jesus provided to the disciples, and this help dwells in us. Lift your hands and declare, "Holy Spirit, `I thank you for being my help."

We must also pattern our conduct to resemble that of Christ, as directed by the Holy Spirit. The overarching role of the Holy Spirit is to help us to promote Christ. We re-present Christ and showcase our relationship when we are guided by laws.

Remember, relationship wins every time. In your difficult season commit to a relationship with the King.

Think about this: "How do I remain free?"

Prayer: "*Lord, help me to appreciate what having a relationship with you means.*"

As you navigate through difficult times, may you appreciate the love God has for you and may you bask in the splendour of the relationship which wins every time.

Chapter 2

Pursued by Love

"… Through him God reconciled everything to himself. He made peace with everything in heaven and on earth by means of Christ's blood on the cross. This includes you who were once far away from God. You were his enemies, separated from him by your evil thoughts and actions. Yet now he has reconciled you to himself through the death of Christ in his physical body. As a result, he has brought you into his own presence, and you are holy and blameless as you stand before him without a single fault."(Colossians 1: 20-22 NLT)

Some years ago, while preparing my sermon to share at a Good Friday service, I ran into my father-in law who engaged me in an interview as he normally would. "What will be the subject of your message?" he asked. Eagerly I responded, "I want to share about the redemption of Jesus Christ; however, I cannot seem to come up with the right analogy that will leave my audience thinking". "Hahaha!!", he chuckled as usual. "Son, what Christ did on the cross was remarkable and does not need any sensationalism. Think of God's redemption plan like this." He proceeded to share a story with me about a little boy called Johnny. Johnny lived in a deep rural community with his father, a carpenter. During the summer, while school was out, Johnny would spend time with his dad in his woodwork shop. One day they came up with an impressive idea to create a little boat that they could play with in the nearby stream. So, Johnny and his father constructed the miniature craft from some spare wood in the shop.

Like Johnny and his dad, God the Father, His Son and the Holy Spirit fashioned a masterpiece called man in the genesis of time.

"Then God said, 'Let us make human beings in our image, to be like us. They will reign over the fish in the sea, the birds in the sky, the livestock, all the wild animals on the earth, and the small animals that scurry along the ground.'" (Genesis 1: 26 NLT)

God, being omniscient, carefully thought about man and his wellbeing. He first created a delightful home, Eden, and developed a deliberate project over which man would rule. Having installed the provisions necessary for him He then made man with His own hands.

I want to declare to you that you were carefully thought about, and purposefully constructed. Provisions were ordered in your favour. You are the outcome of God's ideology.

Credited for producing the greatest artwork of all time, man, Jehovah retained the invention along with its patent. God is sometimes referred to as Lord which is translated from the Hebrew word Adonai meaning “owner”. Man’s role as steward of the garden is proof that he was under God’s authority.

“For every house has a builder, but the one who built everything is God.” (Hebrews 3:4NLT)

Unlike Johnny and his father, who merely came up with a random idea to create a boat from unused material in the corner of a shop, God clinically planned, designed, and manufactured His product.

Prayer: “Lord, thank you for making me so wonderfully complex!”

“Your workmanship is marvelous—how well I know it.” (Psalm 139:14NLT)

One day, Johnny took the boat out to play in the nearby stream. Tragically, the unprecedented rushing of the water that afternoon captured the boat and sent it downstream. With all his might, Johnny scampered after it, doing all within his ability to rescue his vessel. Unfortunately, his best efforts proved futile; the boat was lost.

If a boy can disregard the impending danger, to retrieve his lost boat, how much more will our heavenly Father rescue us from despair?

Naturally, Johnny was saddened at the recent occurrences and oh how he longed to be united with his boat again. Can you see a similar picture here with God? Yes, God placed Adam in the Garden of Eden, but he and all humanity one day got lost down the stream of sin. While man was swept away, not because of the incompetence and weakness of God to sustain, but by his own choice, God longed to unite with humanity.

"Still, everyone died—from the time of Adam to the time of Moses—even those who did not disobey an explicit commandment of God, as Adam did. Now Adam is a symbol, a representation of Christ, who was yet to come." (Romans 5: 14 NLT)

Unfortunately, this did not affect Adam only, but all of us were washed down the waterway of sin. I want to declare today that upon your public confession of Jesus Christ as Lord and your unwavering faith in Him as the only way to a relationship with God, you will be delivered from the awful stream of sin.

“When Adam sinned, sin entered the world. Adam’s sin brought death, so death spread to everyone, for everyone sinned.” (Romans 5:12NLT)

Later that year, Johnny attended an Easter celebration at the nearby town. Lacking money to participate in the games with his friends, he strolled down the plaza, window shopping. Astonished, he noticed his boat in the window of a toy shop.

Flabbergasted, he called out to the shopkeeper with tears running down his cheek, “That’s my boat”. The shop keeper responded, “If you want the boat you will have to buy it.”

“But that’s my boat, I made it with my own hands” Johnny contended. The thoughtless shopkeeper insisted, “If you want the boat you have to pay for it.” Disappointed but determined, Johnny ran out to a nearby pub to find his dad. “Dad can I get $50 to purchase my boat?” Johnny pleaded. His father, overcome with compassion and understanding, gave Johnny the money to make the purchase. The boy rushed back to the shop and purchased the boat. With tears freely descending from his eyes but with unspeakable joy in his heart, he shouted, “I own you twice. I created you, I lost you and I bought you again for myself.”

This story paints a picture of what God our father and Christ the Son did for us over 2000 years ago. Having made us and lost us to sin, Christ redeemed us to himself by purchasing us with His own blood.

By this time, I had forgotten that I was preparing a sermon. Tears began to flow, and my heart was filled with gratitude as, for the first time, I heard the redemption story expressed in such a graphic, emotional and yet effective manner. I could identify with the unconditional love of the Father who supported His son's decision to die for an imperfect world.

For this is how God loved the world: He gave his one and only Son, so that everyone who believes in him will not perish but have eternal life. (St John 3:16)

I simply could not fathom what caused Christ to be so selfless that he would descend from His throne of glory to die for a people so sinful and undeserving of His pardon.

For God made Christ, who never sinned, to be the offering for our sin, so that we could be made right with God through Christ. (2 Corinthians 5: 21NLT)

I believe Christ's last declaration, "it is finished", on the cross was making it known that the redemptive work was complete.

Like Johnny, Christ could say, “I owned them twice. I made them and I bought them with my own blood. They are mine”.

Lift your hands and declare with me today: “I am the property of Christ; He owned me twice. He made me and He bought me by His own Blood”.

And you belong to Christ, and Christ belongs to God (1 Corinthians 3:23 NLT)

As you navigate your difficult moments, reflect on the awesome price Christ willingly paid for an unworthy humanity.

Let us pray: “*Lord thank you for creating me. I am grateful that though I got swept away in the stream of sin and resided in the shop of the wicked one, you were willing to pay the redemptive price. Thank you for saving me.*”

Chapter 3

Switch: Take Me Instead

For no one can ever be made right with God by doing what the law commands. The law simply shows us how sinful we are. (Romans 3: 20)

I recently became aware of an incident involving a little boy named James. He was a 6th grader who rarely attended school and when he did, he was often bullied. Obviously hungry one day at school, James found his way into the cafeteria and stole a pizza. Just as he was about to make his escape, the chef entered the kitchen and accosted him, "You little thief, come here!" James was fetched like a fish caught in a net and immediately brought to the headmaster, Mr Black. It was a known fact that if anyone was caught stealing, the procedure was to escort them to the open area in front of the school. The perpetrator would then be stripped of his shirt, bent over on the famous wooden bench and the infamous prescribed treatment for wrongdoing administered.

The school corridors generally became the grandstand of a classic show down as the procedure was carried out for all to witness. Have you ever reflected on the upshot of sin?

Paul wrote," For the wages of sin is death," (Romans 6:23 NLT)

The consequence of our failure to uphold the laws of God is eternal demise. As with James in the story above, we should have been relieved of our coat and exposed for our wrongdoing. We should be led to the halls of condemnation and given the full effect of rejection; the harshest treatment reserved for transgressors. No amount of good done can right past wrongs. Our failure to live to the standard required was the prerequisite for the most painful outcome. Bitterness, sadness, misery, and hopelessness is salary earned from a minute's work of sin.

Pray with me: *"God help me to reflect on the impact of sin so much that I will evade every chance presented to violate your expectation."*

As anticipated, James was asked to remove his shirt and bent over on the little wooden bench positioned in front of the chief administrator. The evidence of hardship, struggle and sufferings was evident on James' back. The bones were visible, his ribs were piercing through his skin. This is a clear imagery of how humanity was viewed by God. Like James, we were marked with helplessness, hopelessness, bitterness, misery, and sufferings, all effects of the virus of sin. We deserved our pay for the work we executed knowingly, or unknowingly.

Evil people get rich for the moment, but the reward of the godly will last. (Proverbs 11:18NLT)

As the principal was about to punish James for the offence committed, another boy cried out, "No sir! Beat me instead". The boy continued, "He cannot manage another whopping; please I'll take his place on the bench." The boy's compassion reminds me of what Jesus did for failed humanity.

But he was pierced for our rebellion, crushed for our sins. He was beaten so we could be whole. He was whipped so we could be healed. (Isaiah 53:5NLT)

He did not try to persuade the persecutor to look beyond our wrongs; rather, He said, "Take me instead. Sin must be hung on a tree but take me instead. They are guilty and deserve to die but they will never be able to live through eternal damnation. Take me instead."

"He personally carried our sins in his body on the cross so that we can be dead to sin and live for what is right. By his wounds you are healed." (1 Peter 2: 24 NLT)

It was a fact that James failed by stealing the pizza, but the condition of his body moved another student to take his place. Too many times, people are treated without mercy because of mistakes they made years ago. This story illustrates the compassionate heart of Jesus Christ to us.

Undoubtedly, we failed significantly and deserved the worst but instead we were given the best.

"For everyone has sinned; we all fall short of God's glorious standard." (Romans 3: 23 NLT)

Like Joe, Christ took our place of judgment, condemnation, death, and destruction, showcasing the depth of God's mercy towards humanity.

"For his unfailing love toward those who fear him is as great as the height of the heavens above the earth." (Psalm 103: 11)

Lift your hands and declare: "Hallelujah! Hallelujah! Hallelujah! Thank you for your mercies that are new daily."

I want to declare, "it is of the LORD's mercies that we are not consumed, because His compassions fail not. They are new every morning: great is thy faithfulness." [Lamentation 3:23]

Grace is the free, unmerited and undeserved favor of God that we were incapable of earning. It was awarded purely out of love for an imperfect world.

St John 3:16 "For God so loved the world that he gave His only begotten Son that whosoever believeth in him should not perish but have everlasting life."

Reading this book today, you may be that person who is or knows someone who is an adulterer, rapist, sorcerer, murderer, thief, abortionist, homosexual or any other such sinner. Space is available for you, compassion fails not, mercy is renewed, and regeneration can be had. A fresh verdict has been released. Be confident that your sinful, failed, and abortive state qualifies you as one who is able to access the grace of God. Your myriad of failures is not a roadblock to grace. The multiplicity of wrongs can be covered with three simple steps:

- Admit
- Believe
- Commit

"If you confess with your mouth the Lord Jesus, and shalt believe in your heart that God has raised Him from the dead, you will be saved." (Romans 10:9NLT)

It is not possible to go so far that you are beyond redemption. The unconditional, seemingly reckless love of God has granted infinite grace and mercy for even the foulest sinner.

"He has removed our sins as far from us as the east is from the west." (Psalm 103:12NLT)

As you navigate this journey, walk with pride, and hold your head up high knowing that Jesus exclaimed, "Take me instead." Be committed to the relationship with Christ no matter what. It was Christ who shouted, "Take me instead".

Pray this prayer with me: *"Lord I am a sinner and am guilty of transgressing your laws. I believe you died on the cross to redeem me. I commit serving you hereafter. Amen."*

Chapter 4

Reject the Stretcher

For you know that when your faith is tested, your endurance has a chance to grow. (James 1: 3NLT)

While our faith is tested through trials, faith is not produced from trials. The testing of our faith through trials reveals the depth and sincerity of the faith we possess. This ongoing testing produces patience to trust God in even more difficult circumstances. Your testing will produce a more updated, current, and relevant believer.

Pray this prayer with me: "*Lord help me to withstand the testing of my faith even in the most difficult moments of my life. Amen.*"

Being an avid Olympic fan, I often engage in studying the life of current and past sporting superstars. One of my recent investigations yielded the epic testimonial of Derek Redmond, a former British athlete.

God will publish a story worthy of exploring when you persevere through your difficult times producing a testimony of faith that was tried.

Leading up to the 1992 Olympics, Derek Redmond was favored to win the 400m race for men. He was constantly improving his time and showing great potential to even set a new world record. The preparations for the Olympic games required much commitment and dedication to execute the strenuous drills stipulated by his coach. So it is with believers: we should treat each day as an opportunity to excel when our faith is tested and thus be committed to studying God's word, praying to God, and worshipping the Living God. We should never take our assignments for granted. See it as an occasion to please God through faith.

Then we apostles can spend our time in prayer and teaching the word. (Acts 6: 4NLT)

No doubt Derek was a disciplined chap who loved the Olympic Games and saw it as an honorable prospect to represent his country on the world scene.

How many times do we treat God's assignment with disdain?

I challenge you to resist to teach, preach, sing another song or serve in any other capacity until you have examined your heart for possible defects.

Pray this prayer: *"Lord help me to treat every assignment honorably"*.

When I was growing up in Jamaica, a Bible verse often used by my mother was, "When you think it is peace and safety, sudden destruction comes upon you." Derek Redmond's commitment to his assignment was tested. Within a few months prior to the world staging he had endured eight (8) surgeries. For many persons this would be reason enough to give up, but for Derek, he was resolute in making it to the games. As he did, *we* will encounter difficulties at varying intervals in our lives, but we must commit to honoring God despite the odds.

Endure suffering along with me, as a good soldier of Christ Jesus. (2 Timothy 2: 3 NLT)

Declare today: "I will not give up! I refuse to stop! I will not give in to external pressures. I will fight the good fight of faith as a good soldier of Jesus Christ."

Derek's persistence earned him the right to be a participant at the 1992 Olympic Games.

I declare that your intentional pursuit of God will yield you a position in 'breakthrough lane'.

Feeling excited and accomplished, Derek could hardly wait for the shooter's gun to explode. "On Your mark, get set…'' Bam! All the athletes were sent on their way. In less than 50 seconds Derek crossed the finish line in the first round of the qualifiers. To his amazement, not only did he win his heat, but he ran the fastest time in the qualifying rounds. Finally, things seemed to have been changing for Derek. Sometimes, after a complicated period, a break comes. While you celebrate, be cognizant that all seasons have an expiry date.

Derek again lined up, this time for the quarter finals, waiting for the shooter's gun. People were cheering all over the stadium, blowing vuvuzelas and chanting "Derek! Derek!" as the young promising athlete was only 400 metres away from the medal podium.

People will shout the loudest for you when excellence is guaranteed but as they scream for you in favorable seasons so they will become derisive when tragedy strikes. Discern the cheerers from the jeerers!

Pray with me: *"Lord open my eyes and enable me to discern those who are truly my help".*

The gun went off and as expected, Derek was off to a quick start with the field trailing him but suddenly, tragedy struck, and Derek went down holding his leg. The supporters in the stands groaned in disappointment while the medical staff made their way towards the stricken athlete. To everyone's surprise, he got up and started hopping towards the finish line. For many this was ridiculous; the race was already won. Derek's assignment in this game was to complete his course. Many times, we view our assignment through a competitive eye rather than the desire to finish.

A couple of years ago, I failed to meet the required standard for high school graduation and thus was not allowed to walk down the aisle. I managed to earn a gift card-size, grey and white certificate, being successful in only three of my final exams. Despite my being one of the top students in the school, no one paid attention to the real reason for my frequent absences which prevented me from excelling the way I should. I had suffered a head injury that almost took my life and had to spend weeks in the hospital; the cheerers became quiet. Not one of my teachers or even my principal visited me in hospital, but I was awarded the distasteful certificate. When you need the cheerers most, they will often become quiet.

Despite falling out of the race, today I am one of the most accomplished of my cohort. Don't stop! Keep going. In the words of the late Dr. Martin Luther King Jr, "If you can't run, walk. If you can't walk, crawl but whatever you do see to it that you keep moving."

The fastest runner doesn't always win the race, the strongest warrior doesn't always win the battle.

The wise sometimes go hungry, and the skillful are not necessarily wealthy. And those who are educated don't always lead successful lives. It is all decided by chance, by being in the right place at the right time. (Ecclesiastes 9:11NLT)

Declare this with me: "I will not stop; I will hop if I need to, but I will not stop."

The first- aiders tried to persuade Derek Redmond to get on the stretcher but he refused. He yelled "I came here to complete the race and I am going to do that".

The stretcher was not just a medical tool capable of aiding to escort Derek to the sideline. It represented that instrument that would put an end to whatever chance remained for Derek to complete the race. Derek knew if he accepted a few minutes ride to the sideline the organizers would call the race over but as long as he stayed on the track , he still had an opportunity to fulfil his life's goal of completing the race.

Think about this: What are some stretchers that are available to us, making us abort our mission?

Could it be doubt, past failure, disappointment, fear, illness, unforgiveness, and stress.

Declare with me: "I reject every stretcher that is made available to hinder progress, block vision, and destabilize me in my quest to fulfill my purpose."

Soon after a loud uproar could be heard from the stands. A man started to push past the security and made his way onto the track: it was Derek's father. He rushed to aid his son along the journey.

If an earthly father can break protocol to assist his son in his difficult time, how much so our eternal father?

God is our refuge and strength, always ready to help in times of trouble. (Psalm 46:1NLT)

As with Derek's father who was seated in the stands, so our heavenly father is positioned in the VIP section cheering us along. Should we become overwhelmed, he will make himself visible.

When you go through deep waters, I will be with you. When you go through rivers of difficulty, you will not drown. When you walk through the fire of oppression, you will not be burned up; the flames will not consume you. (Isaiah 43:2NLT)

Our God is not only present but commits to navigate us through our difficult times.

Something interesting transpired. As soon as Derek was a few meters away from the finish line, his father pulled back, leaving him to get to the line while he looked on. In order for us to grow and triumph, our heavenly father sometimes steps back and, with watchful eyes, observes us as we push past our challenges. So that we may overcome and fulfil the assignment, we must refuse the stretcher of the enemy.

As you navigate through difficulties, may you be perceptive to the 'stretchers' that are offered to you, but which will detour and delay you. May you reject all distractions and stay focused to stay the course

Let us pray: "God reveal to me every stretcher that is being used by the enemy to prevent me from fulfilling my purpose. Help me to define my goal as is outlined in your will and to pursue relentlessly. Amen."

Chapter 5

Use the Name (Username)

The name of the Lord is a strong fortress; the godly run to Him and are safe. (Proverbs 18:10 NLT)

A few years ago, while I served as an infantry man in the army, I had a mind-blowing experience. Once, soon after I was posted on duty, it began to rain profusely. The camping site I was at is generally known for its vulnerability to flooding even with the lightest of showers. In a matter of minutes, the water rose so high that I had to use several concrete blocks to create a platform to elevate myself. After about 30 minutes I had to relocate to a new area in the camp because of the terrible, persistent overflow. The flood waters were so aggressive, it became a hazard for even a trained military man to maneuver, so I decided to make my way back to the guardroom. En route, I heard a voice crying out in the dark, "Souljie! Help!". From a distance, it sounded like the voice of a young woman. Suddenly, I remembered that there was an area below the camp that is frequently inundated when it rains and is therefore made impassable. Without thinking about the consequences, I rushed to the "colour store", snatched a roll of rope, tied one end to my waist and the other to a light pole at the side of the camp and sprinted towards the direction of the sound.

If a mortal, imperfect stranger can be touched with the needs of an absolute stranger, how much more our heavenly father?

This High Priest of ours understands our weaknesses, for he faced all of the same testing we do, yet he did not sin. (Hebrews 4:15 NLT)

God not only loves us, but he cares about the issues we face and thus makes himself available to be our help regardless of our socioeconomic, educational, religious or political status.

In my desperation I prayed, and the Lord listened; He saved me from all my troubles.

(Psalm 34: 6 NLT)

Sometimes, we think of God as being too remote to rescue, too far away to hear, too busy to be concerned, and too holy to regard us. The writer of the Psalm attempts to convince us "God is our refuge and strength, always ready to help in times of trouble." (Psalm 46:1NLT)

When there is an emergency, the tendency is to call 911 and wait for help to arrive. Not so with God: He is already present.

Pray with me: *"I will call on you God for I know you are close enough to respond, concerned enough to act, and faithful enough to give me an expected end."*

Although it was dark, lonely and dangerous I was compelled to hearken to the request. To hear a need in the kingdom and not respond is unpardonable.

If a simple, dispensable, mortal man can uphold a principle of the kingdom even in grave danger, how much so the sovereign God who is unflinching.

St Matthew 7:7 outlines "ask and it shall be given."

God will not ignore a cry for help, especially when the name Jesus is used. … so that the Father will give you whatever you ask for, using my name. (St John 15: 16B NLT)

I got to the car and managed to rescue the occupants, all because someone decided to use the name "Soujie".

There is a name that is above every other name that when used releases healing, deliverance, provision, protection, and any other need that you may possess. This name is an all-purpose name. This name is Jesus.

For "Everyone who calls on the name of the Lord will be saved. (Romans 10:13 NLT)

In order to enter an Information Technology secure environment, one needs the correct username and the matching password. The protected environment can be accessed by citizens who have the appropriate log-in details.

It is interesting that David, when faced with a firewall called Goliath, gathered the password consisting of five characters (stones) F.A.I.T.H. and entered it into a security window (his sling). Prior to this he entered the username 'JESUS'. "You come to me with a sword and a spear, But I come to you in the name of the Lord of host." The release was made, and blockage was removed allowing open access to David and the people of Israel.

Lift your hands and declare: "Jesus! Jesus! Jesus!" by faith.

As with the woman in the car, who refused to die without making an attempt to call on the name capable of providing the help needed, you can use that name as often as you need. Results are in that name. It is illogical to suffer under the lies of the enemy and not use the name of Jesus.

The writer in Proverbs 18:10 announced that the LORD's name is a strong tower capable of providing a "safe haven" for the righteous. While all are delivered when they call on the name of the Lord, a special accommodation is made for the righteous, those made right through faith in Jesus Christ. Safe, as translated from the Hebrew word sawgab, means to be elevated so high that hostility become ineffective.

May every hostility affecting you, your family, your household be rendered powerless in the name of Jesus.

No weapon turned against you will succeed. You will silence every voice raised up to accuse you. These benefits are enjoyed by the servants of the Lord; their vindication will come from me. I, the Lord, have spoken! (Isaiah 54:17NLT)

Chapter 6

Trust the Process

Our difficult times often open the door for us to blame people, situations, and things. Do not walk through that door, as it may be a bait to depression, frustration, sorrow or even anger. Each step forms one component of the finished product. You cannot have an end product- your purpose - if you fail to assemble all the components called experiences.

Paul charged the worried Christians amidst persecution … And we know that God causes everything to work together for the good of those who love God and are called according to his purpose for them. (Romans 8: 28NLT)

The loving God will allow those who love him and are walking in His will to have varying experiences, bad or good. Note however, that these experiences are intentional. There is no experience that you have that was merely a mistake. It was all a part of God's divine plan to finish the work that His son announced was finished on the cross. If we say that God is the all-knowing God, we must accept that there is nothing foreign to Him.

Some years ago, my cousin decided to enter The National Draught's Competition and as usual sought my opinion on how I thought he would perform. Now, I knew my cousin was an awesome player being adept at the game. He had no match in our local community, but this was the national league. I knew he was the don of Draught in our little village but there were not many educated persons there, so the truth is I was not sure.

Similarly, how many times do we treat God as a local don who is capable of conquering in small battles but when it comes to the big things, we are not so convinced?

After thinking about my cousin's track record of success, I finally told him I believed he would do well. God has a perfect track record of destroying enemy territories, providing for His people, cursing sicknesses, resurrecting the dead, commanding even things without ears, and sustaining His troops.

May your minds and hearts discern the unsearchable revelation of God.

Pray with me: *"I believe you can and will do anything. Amen"*

The finals of the Draughts competition resonate with me to this very day. My cousin was up against one of the best players in the entire Caribbean. Not only was he a good player but he had a bachelor's degree in Law. I thought to myself, "this boy must know the entire law of the game of draughts. The match was exceptionally intense, and I could see the nail-biting emotions on the faces of all those watching.

Our perceptions of a thing often magnify it into a monstrous problem. We must combat this through praising God.

Come, let us tell of the Lord's greatness; let us exalt his name together. (Psalm 34:3)

Five minutes into the game and no one appeared to be losing, then bam! My cousin made what seemed to be a silly move and allowed the opponent to take two of his counters. You could see the smirk on the up-and-coming lawyer's face. Feeling a bit disheartened, I thought to myself "I'll just go sit down around the back and wait until they are done".

Comparably, how many times do we give up on God just because our prayers seem go unanswered?

It is easy to trust when the tides flow to our advantage. However, in times of opposition we tend to cry, worry and doubt, eventually giving up on God like I gave up on my cousin.

David expressed a similar experience when he too asked: "Why am I discouraged? Why is my heart so sad?" (Psalm 42: 5 NLT)

Some may argue that it was bad to question God, but what would have been worse is if David had lost faith in God. The Psalmist continues, "I will put my hope in God! I will praise him again". Note, David took immediate action when he recognized the enemy's stronghold: fear, worry and doubt. He launched the missiles of hope and praise to ravage the very habitat of the foe.

Hope is translated from the ancient Hebrew word "yachal" which means to expect. Always expect the draughts man El Elohim to come through for you.

Stop toying with the enemy, respond urgently with your most lethal weapons: hope and praise.

Praise in this scripture is derived from the Hebrew word "yadah" which means to give thanks and to laud. In your most challenging moment, do not forget to show gratitude and to boast about the incredibility of our 'draughts man' El Gibor, the strong and mighty in battle.

Pray with me: *"Lord I expect you to respond to my difficulties according to your sovereignty"*.

As I was about to walk away from the draughts table, I heard 'bam! bam! bam! bam! It was a four-take by my cousin that awarded him a king. The little crowd from my village started to rejoice. In two minutes, the game was over, and my cousin emerged the champion. As was the case with me, we often find it difficult to stand firm and believe in our draughts man. David knew his draughts man and trusted him to defeat the bear and the lion.

It is better to take refuge in the Lord than to trust in people. (Psalm 118:8)

He was committed to trusting this same draughts player in order to defeat Goliath. Different game, same treatment; my God is the Greatest Draughts player.

David replied to the Philistine, "You come to me with sword, spear, and javelin, but I come to you in the name of the Lord of Heaven's Armies—the God of the armies of Israel, whom you have defied.

(1 Samuel 17:45-46 NLT)

We must recognize Him as the great and astute draughts player who sometimes allows us to go down paths where we appear to lose. The process of losing may entail, but is not limited to, job losses, health, loss of loved ones or failed business ventures. What have you lost so valuable that a capable God cannot give better?

One of the names used to refer to God is El Shalom which means the God of peace. In ancient Hebrew, names were more than just labels used to distinguish between individuals. The word from which El Shalom is derived is "shem" which implies the nature and characteristics of 'El Elyon.' The nature of God is to bring peace where chaos reigns.

How can God be peace yet there is so much disaster, wickedness, and chaos in our world? Peace as translated from Shalom does not merely mean absence of war but rather restitution.

Rest assured that you may lose for a season, but you will be restored.

So after you have suffered a little while, he will restore, support, and strengthen you, and he will place you on a firm foundation. (1 Peter 5: 10 NLT)

God permits seasonal losses to rebuild, restore, strengthen and promote His people.

Declare this with me: "Lord thank you for my low seasons. You are unflinching and therefore know no danger. It is impossible for you to fail."

A good leader will sometimes lead his subordinates into paths that may seem unfavourable, from the perspective of the follower, but be confident it will work out to their benefit.

The Lord directs the steps of the godly. He delights in every detail of their lives. (Psalm 37:23NLT)

As explained in Psalm 23, those steps may be beside the still waters WHERE YOU MAY THINK THERE ARE NO BLESSINGS, or in the green pastures where abundance of favor resides. Sometimes those steps may even lead to the valley of the shadow of death a place of no progress. As you navigate difficult times, be reminded that there are no mistakes so great to undo the plans that are within the will of God.

Surely your goodness and unfailing love will pursue me all the days of my life. (Psalm 23:6NLT)

Navigating difficult times requires us to trust the process.

Prayer*: "Dear Lord, please help me to trust the process knowing that you are working things out according to your perfect will."*

Chapter 7

Rest assured; you will not diminish

Build homes, and plan to stay. Plant gardens and eat the food they produce. Marry and have children. Then find spouses for them so that you may have many grandchildren. Multiply! Do not dwindle away (Jeremiah 29:5-6 NLT)

One of the most common responses to a challenging situation is the desire for its immediate termination or removal.

"If only the problem could be removed, I would know that God is with me." Difficult times are not an indication of an absent God but a reassurance of the committed God.

Don't be discouraged, for I am your God. I will strengthen you and help you. I will hold you up with my victorious right hand. (Isaiah 41:10 NLT)

God's plan for his children in Jeremiah 29 was to purify Israel through the period of exile. Your difficult time is a period of pruning and not eternal imprisonment. God will not alter the cleansing process to prove the proximity of his presence. Rather than praying for an instant end, ask God to perfect his will in your life.

Declare with me: "Your will is perfect, your ways are just, you are righteous in all you do."

Deliverance from a situation is not always an extracted elevation out of, or an instant end to, oppression. Sometimes God wants to promote endurance and showcase His ability to sustain in hardships. Paul an apostle of the Lord, credited for writing approximately fourteen of the twenty-seven books of the New Testament, was afflicted with an uncomfortable thorn in the flesh. He prayed three times for deliverance but was still unable to persuade God to alter His divine will. We are instruments created for God's glory; thus, He reserves the right to make the final ruling.

Each time He said, "My grace is all you need. My power works best in weakness." So now I am glad to boast about my weaknesses, so that the power of Christ can work through me. (2 Corinthians 12:9NLT)

Like Paul, let us swiftly accept God's divine will and declare, "Most gladly will I rather glory in my infirmities, that the power of Christ may rest upon me."

The people of God were reluctant to build houses and have children despite being told they would spend 70 years in exile.

Think about this: How many times do you sink into depression because your problems fail to be resolved immediately?

During difficult times people often project their focus on the issues and not on the purpose. Missing what God is doing in your difficult season is equally as dangerous as not knowing God. Do not live like prisoners in an enclosed area that is meant for perfecting God's will in you. It was in prison that Paul and Silas offered up prayers that erupted into worship and invited the presence of God which shook the stronghold open and dismantled the shackles and the yokes of bondage.

May your tenacity to honour, in spite of imprisonment, move God to respond favourably.

Pray with me: *"In my difficult condition, show me your divine intent. Hear my plea Lord. Help me to not miss what you are doing in this season, simply because I am trapped trying to escape."*

God's vision for the people was that they would multiply, increase, and grow in Babylon as they did in Egypt. How many times do you wish you were still going to high school, still single, or still in your 30s when faced with a difficult season?

You are a seed that can grow in any environment regardless of the season. A shift in location or a change in time cannot alter your God-intended purpose. The same God who kept you in a previous setting, reigns in this season. Grow into that fruitful tree you were fashioned to be.

Lift your hands and declare with me: "I am a seed and I possess growth capabilities. I will bloom wherever I am planted, and I will produce good fruits."

The sustenance, care and nourishment of the seed is the role of the Husbandman, our Father. It is illegal for a father to not provide, guide, and protect His seed.

I am the true grapevine, and my Father is the gardener. (St John 15:1 NLT)

The word Father is derived from the Greek word "Pater" signifying nourisher, protector, and upholder. Rest assured that you will be nourished, protected, and upheld as you navigate the varying seasons.

Pray with me: "*I submit myself as a seed into your care my father. Amen.*"

God desires to prosper you in all areas of your life, inclusive of your soul. He desires to bless you beyond material blessings and physical prosperity.

Seek the Kingdom of God above all else, and live righteously, and he will give you everything you need. (St Matthew 6:33)

Note however, that our loving father is more concerned about the status of your soul than he is about delivering earthly requests.

Dear friend, I hope all is well with you and that you are as healthy in body as you are strong in spirit. (3 John 1:2NLT)

May you pursue God relentlessly and not His hand (what he can do).

As citizens of the kingdom of heaven dwelling in the capacity of resident aliens in the earthly realm, we are expected to impact our environment.

You are the salt of the earth. But what good is salt if it has lost its flavor? Can you make it salty again? It will be thrown out and trampled underfoot as worthless. (St Matthew 5:13NLT)

God's objective was for them to do good in the towns, cities, and nation of Babylon. Someone is depending on you to navigate your difficult season. By submitting to the will of God, they will encounter Christ. You are a seed and you should grow wherever you are planted.

May you begin to appreciate your season and prosper in every moment of your life.

In your season of elevation, you will encounter distractors - some as prophets - who will encourage you to act contrary to the word of God. Listening to the wrong source may result in you diminishing in a season of progress, growth, and development.

This is what the Lord of Heaven's Armies, the God of Israel, says: *"Do not let your prophets and fortune-tellers who are with you in the land of Babylon trick you. Do not listen to their dreams, because they are telling you lies in my name. I have not sent them," says the Lord. This is what the Lord says: "You will be in Babylon for seventy years. But then I will come and do for you all the good things I have promised, and I will bring you home again.* (Jeremiah 29:8-10 NLT)

Messages are to be evaluated by the content and the source. Clearly the prophecies presented by the diviners contradicted the Word of God. We can infer that if the Bible is regarded as the highest authority, God will never make another conflicting proclamation. Lastly, God through Jeremiah contends "I have not sent them" clearly suggesting that they were impersonators.

May every impersonator operating in the prophetic realm be exposed and their missives be rendered null and void, in Jesus' name.

As you navigate your difficulties, some of which may seem like exile, may you experience God's blessings. May you, according to His will, enjoy the prosperity of His hand in every way.

Declare this with me: God, I believe the plans you have, for I know they are thoughts of peace and not of evil. I am confident that they have been fashioned with the intention of giving me an expected end. I will not be diminished in Jesus' name.

Chapter 8

It must cost me something

But the king replied to Araunah, "No, I insist on buying it, for I will not present burnt offerings to the Lord my God that have cost me nothing." So David paid him fifty pieces of silver for the threshing floor and the oxen. (2 Samuel 24:24NLT)

David, though regarded as a great king among his compatriots in the earthly realm, refused to accept a gift that cost him nothing to dedicate to the King who reigns over both the Earth and the Heavens. We must endeavor to offer the best worship, regardless of the season. Whether you navigate difficult times or not, your worship should cost you everything.

During my early years as a Christian, I learnt of a man in a neighboring church called Mr John. He was a passionate worshipper who was branded as being very loud. Mr John's favourite chorus was "when I think of the goodness of Jesus and all that he has done for me, my soul cries out hallelujah. Thank God for saving me". Songs of that type would cause him to become emotional as he reflected upon his past of drugs, alcohol, gambling and an untold number of misdeeds. His expressions included groaning, shouting, crying, and even running. Clearly, the product of praise reflected the content of his heart. Often, our worship is relegated to a reaction to a worship tune, our contribution to a ministry, and our distinct ability to unleash our tongues in service. These acts, though included in worship, are merely expressions of worship, which is an output of the heart.

For God is Spirit, so those who worship him must worship in spirit and in truth. (John 4:24NLT)

True worship will cost you something. What is your worship costing you? True worship sees God as the same in lack and in excess, in good and in bad. True worship is marked by intense and intentional submission coupled with deliberate honor bred out of extravagant love for the living God.

Let us pray: "Lord help me evaluate the way in which worship you; let my worship be sincere."

Sincere adoration is recognized when there is a deliberate aim to make God the priority in one's life, despite the circumstances. Complete obeisance is manifested as a practice of our everyday life and expressed in a myriad of ways to include gratefulness.

I want to declare that your heart and mind will agree with your mouth and your expressions will be pure.

Rest assured, the genuineness of your worship will be tested, sometimes by the most unlikely source. Anything that is true can withstand scrutiny.

Not, long after, Mr John's genuineness re worship was tested. One day after service, his pastor asked to speak with him. "Mr John, how are you doing?" he asked.

"I'm well pastor, how are you?" Mr John replied.

The pastor responded, "Mr John I'm well, thank you. Next week we will be having my pastor's appreciation service. I know you tend to shout, but we will be having the international overseer as guest speaker. Please do not shout and if possible, do not bother to express yourself in the usual way. I also know your passion for good pumpkin soup so if you can do me this small favour, I will have a lovely bowl prepared for you next week after service".

What is affecting your worship in this season? What is causing you to withhold honest worship from God?

I declare every weapon, be it physical or spiritual, that is hampering your worship, powerless in the name of Jesus. I declare that you were formed to worship, and no high or low thing will hinder that in this season or any other season.

Difficult times often produce several factors that may discourage true and sincere worship. Broken relationships, rocky marriages and unemployment sometimes increase the cost, making it unaffordable to the worshipper. When this happens, shift the focus to the worthiness of God and not the wealth of His hand. Honoring God's previous and present successes is good but worshipping Him who is worthy is of more value.

Psalm 96:7 (NKJV) Give to the LORD, O families of the people. Give to the LORD glory and strength. Give to the LORD the glory due His name.

The writer of Psalm 96 emphasizes the need to credit God the glory He deserves. May your style of worship change drastically to reflect a surrendered heart filled with love. May your worship be of such potency that you will offer it even in life's worst storm. Your worship must be a gift borne out of the worthiness of God and not His ability to respond to prayers. Such attitude to worship will weather a storm of any magnitude.

Give to the Lord the glory he deserves! Bring your offering and come into his presence.

Worship the Lord in all his holy splendor. (1 Chronicles 16: 29 NLT)

Mr John thought about the request and then measured it against His love for soup. He reasoned with himself, "I love worship, but I can worship at another time. God knows I am not perfect, and times are hard. Most times, I do not have anything to eat anyways so I believe God with all His mercies will pardon me". He finally agreed to sit quietly in church quietly for the price of a bowl soup. How many times do we put off a seemingly less urgent God for a more demanding situation? God is worth more than all the wealth in the world. Your worship should cost you everything.

Let all that I am praise the Lord; with my whole heart, I will praise his holy name (Psalm 103: 1 NTL)

It cost God everything, to make a believer out of a sinner. Our worship should mirror John 3:16. God gave His only begotten son (Everything) to die for a sinful world (Selfless giving). Worship must be selfless and cost us everything.

Let us pray: *"I confess that my worship has not always been selfless; sometimes it is conditional, offered only in favorable seasons. There are days when I worship for the camera. Please forgive me and help me to give my best to you in sincerity."*

The following Sunday, the pastor made sure to make eye contact with Mr John to remind him of the terms and conditions of the unwritten contract. Mr John took his favourite seat in the church but groaned uncontrollably in discomfort throughout the worship session, doing his utmost best to keep quiet. Finally, the preacher was introduced to the little wooden podium and commenced his sermon with Mr John's favourite song. Suddenly, Mr John jumped to his feet and declared, "Soup or no soup hallelujah!"

I want to declare over you blessing or no blessing, healing or no healing, wealth or no wealth, marriage or no marriage, Hallelujah.

There is nothing worth substituting for worship that is due to God. Worship is having an overgenerous love for God, offered through complete submission on non-negotiable terms. It must cost you everything.

God, who is unimaginably sovereign, chooses to regard our gifts but that is not the pledge of worship. It is wrong to assume that your empty shouts and windmill waves can acquire God's attention. Your worship must cost you something. Worship that costs will attract the promise allotted to worship.

Before the Lord, for he is coming! He is coming to judge the earth. He will judge the world with justice, and the nations with his truth. (Psalm 96: 13 NLT)

Costly worship will invite the Holy God to evaluate one's heart, and to provide feedback for improvement. In fact, it is worship that should remodel us to look like the man God created in His own Image. Worship will cost you severed ties with some of the dearest things, people, and systems. True worship costs.

May you, as you navigate your difficult times, realise that God is deserving of the highest form of worship, worship that costs us everything.

Let us pray: *"Lord help me to have a heart like thine. Come and inspect my heart today. I crave your feedback. Give me strength and the will so that I can be reflect you. Amen".*

Chapter 9

Listen in your Wilderness

Then the LORD came and stood there, calling as before, "Samuel! Samuel!" And Samuel answered, "Speak, for Your servant is listening." (1 Samuel 3: 10 NLT)

God is always speaking but we are not always listening. As Eli helped his ward Samuel to recognize the importance of acknowledging and becoming attentive to a sovereign God, so must we quieten our hearts and listen to God for divine instructions.

Let us pray: "*Lord help me to be attentive to you. Speak to me so I can know your ways".*

If I were to interview a group of people asking them; "When you think of the wilderness, what comes to mind? They would probably respond like this:

"The wilderness is an austere, hot, dry, dusty, hard, and forbidding place." Another may say, "the wilderness may be characterized as a lonely, thirsty, and unpleasant place." Some may even describe the wilderness as a place lacking progress, growth, and development. Others may envision the wilderness to be an abandoned space that is barren, without trees or springs, lacking shelter, and incapable of providing food. I am almost certain that not one person would consider the wilderness to be a favorable setting for a picnic, a honeymoon, an anniversary celebration or even a birthday stroll. Yet this is the place that the Lord selected to celebrate two of the most significant milestones for the Israelites: the grand exodus from Egyptian bondage and the remarkable swallowing up of the Pharaoh and his army at the Red Sea.

So, God led them in a roundabout way through the wilderness toward the Red Sea. Thus, the Israelites left Egypt like an army ready for battle. (Exodus 13:18NLT)

According to the Cambridge Dictionary, "the wilderness is an area of land that has not been used to grow crops or had towns and roads built on it, especially because it is difficult to live in as a result of its extremely cold or hot weather or bad earth."

Why on earth would a loving God choose to lead his people whom He loves into the wilderness, a place with the description outlined above?

God is the greatest teacher and, as with all teachers, He has some choice classroom settings, the wilderness being one of His favorites. An effective lesson is measured by its objectives, the learning activities, the assessment, and the feedback. God's objective in this lesson was to educate Israel on who He is.

Hearing and reading about God are not the same as knowing God. The verb 'know' is coined from an ancient Greek word called 'Ginosko'. 'Ginosko' means to come to know, recognize, understand through experience.

The professor God, knew that the best way to get Israel to know who He is, was to take them to a place that lacked food, water, order, comfort, entertainment, and peace. Like Israel, we are sometimes enrolled in God's Experimental course called the Wilderness: Do you know God? These wildernesses include loss of loved ones, illnesses, viruses and job losses, tragedy, loneliness, conflict, hardships, problems, and separations, all of which carry psychological, mental, physical and emotional effects. These effects are disappointments, fear, doubt, stress, unhappiness, depression. They push us into a state of dependency, highlighting our inferiority to a sovereign God. Wildernesses appear for a season, a reason, and a lesson.

What lesson are you learning from your wilderness?

For this objective to be satisfied, God had to choose effective learning activities. He knew that it was only a matter of time before Israel would cry out "Master, we have to food". Then the teacher would step in and demonstrate to the class that he is Jehovah Jireh the God who provides. The Master Rabbi appointed the 'head boy' Moses to strike the rock demonstrating that he is the Living Water. To dispel chaos, He gave 'star boy' Moses, the 10 commandments to guide the students into all truths, showing forth his characteristic as "The Word". He punished those who sinned, thus teaching them that he is the Righteous Judge.

What are you learning in your wilderness?

Contrary to what many may think, the wilderness is a HOLY place. 'Holy', when translated from the Greek word 'Hagios', means to be made clean or set apart.

Notice:

- it was in the wilderness that God gave His law, the word. [Exodus 20]
- it was there he provided manna [Exodus 16]
- it was in that desolate place he fed Elijah by ravens [1 Kings 17:6]
- It was in the wilderness he called Moses into ministry [Exodus 3]

In concretizing a well taught lesson, the teacher God, must carry out an assessment to assess the extent to which the students grasp the concepts. This will determine if the lesson is to be retaught or if movement or progress to the next stage can be made.

Pray with me: *"Lord help me to show forth that which I have learnt about God from my wilderness. Help me to embrace my wilderness to listen as God speaks. Speak Lord! Thy servant heareth."*

Some of us can testify that it was in one of these trying moments that we heard the call of the Lord and surrendered. If God is always speaking, why does it take a wilderness for us to hear him? We can reflect on our former imagery of the wilderness: When there is loneliness, discomfort, lack of entertainment and electronic communication, (an absence of internet and smart phones), and dry, dusty conditions, there is a greater dependence on God, as many of these things are merely distractions.

Lift your hands and declare: "There is some good in my wilderness".

Pray with me: "*Lord please reveal the good lessons to be learnt from my wilderness*".

The wilderness is the place that reveals the absolute need for the true and living God and the stupidity of man to think we can live without God. Man, without God is nothing; God without man is still God. We stand more to benefit from a life dedicated in pursuit of the righteous God.

Search for the Lord and for his strength; continually seek him. (1 Chronicles 16:11)

Finally, a good teacher will not terminate a lesson without providing meaningful evaluation to the class.

Wilderness is derived from the Hebrew word ‘midbar’ which comes from the root word ‘dabar’. ‘Dabar’ means to speak, therefore wilderness can be summarized as the place where God speaks. The wilderness is the place where God’s voice is heard. As you navigate difficult times, embrace your wilderness as this is the place in which God tends to speak.

As you navigate your difficult experiences, may you recognize that God is leading you through the wilderness and that He will test you then bless you in your wilderness experiences.

Chapter 10

Give God Exactly What He Wants

But Samuel replied, "What is more pleasing to the Lord: your burnt offerings and sacrifices or your obedience to his voice. Listen! Obedience is better than sacrifice, and submission is better than offering the fat of rams. (1 Samuel 15: 22 NLT)

'What does God really want?' is perhaps one of the most asked questions throughout the ages.

We have been socialized to think that God merely wants our praises, worship, time, talent, resources and subsequently our lives. This I believe misrepresents the dearest part of God's heart.

"The earth is the Lord's, and everything in it. The world and all its people belong to him." (Psalm 24: 1 NLT)

This amplifies the idea that the very thing you are thinking of giving God is already His. The word 'give' is translated from a Hebrew word 'yahab' meaning to credit or to ascribe. All things tangible and intangible already belong to God. To give then, really means crediting God, the real owner.

Pray with me: "*Lord, I acknowledge you as the one and true owner of all things. Amen.*"

Honor the Lord with your wealth and with the best part of everything you produce. (Proverbs 3: 9 NLT)

The more we give, the more we question ourselves, "Am I giving enough? Am I honoring enough?"

God requires more than your numerical and tangible gifts; he requires your obedience. Samuel, in addressing a similar issue, sought to highlight God's passion for obedience by comparing it with burnt offering. Many times, we treat God as one who can be bought by our gifts. God values obedience over the greatest gifts and sacrifices. Genesis 4 describes an impressive 'show down' where God highlighted His unwavering preference for obedience and a deliberate desire for observance of His instructions. A promising youngster lost his life because his brother provided a sacrifice rather than obeying God's instruction. Too often we get caught up thinking attendance, shouts and money can impress God so much that he turns a blind eye to our disobedience. The prophet Samuel insisted on stating that if God had to choose between gifts and obedience, he would select obedience, all day every day.

May your prayers be answered, and needs addressed, as you walk in obedience to God's word.

The word 'obey', though absent from the Hebrew dictionary, is derived from the word "shema" which means 'to hear'. The word "hear" in Hebrew settings means more than one is listening; it means to move to action, having heard the instruction.

I heard a story years ago about a father and his son Billy living out in Arizona USA. They lived in a well vegetated area. One day Billy was out in the backyard playing when he heard his father yelling, "Billy!".

He responded, "Yeah pop".

The father shouted, "Kneel down and take two steps to your left". Without frowning Billy carried out the instructions as given.

How many times do you wait for clarity before carrying out a God-given instruction? May we become like Billy. Hear, and then move to action.

"Lay down and roll to the left." the father commanded again, and Billy gracefully executed the instructions.

How many times do we get annoyed with those whom God has placed in our lives to guide us particularly when we think instructions are excessive and unfavourable? In our educational training, teachers are taught a good principle: Listen, evaluate, and then act. This principle can be applied to our context. Listen to the instruction, check the source, act immediately. Billy heard his father's instruction clearly and he was confident the instruction was from his father, a reputable source, so he obediently carried out the steps.

May you incline your ear to God, ensure He is the source and move to action on confirmation. Do not put Him off until tomorrow, for tomorrow might be too late.

Pray with me: *"Lord help me to identify your voice, confirm your intent, and execute to perfection*".

"Crawl forward!" the father shouted, and Billy willingly carried out the task.

Billy was confident, that though he did not readily understand, his father was doing this for a good reason. Your Father's intent is to give you an expected end. Embrace the request graciously.

For I know the plans I have for you," says the Lord. "They are plans for good and not for disaster, to give you a future and a hope. (Jeremiah 29:11NLT)

The six- foot man shouted again, "Get up and run towards me!". Billy got up and powered forward as though he was trying out for the 100m national finals.

How diligent are you in being obedient to God? It's easy to remain obedient when you have a mansion in Cherry Gardens, and a Lamborghini in the driveway but what about when health fails, debts increase, and needs arise?

May your desire to obey outweigh your will to defy and reveal the true purpose of your heart.

If you love me, obey my commandments. (John 14:15 NLT)

Billy's dad, happier than a man who recently won the "America's Got Talent" competition would be, pointed to the direction from which his son appeared. "Billy look," he begged. The boy shivered, frightened at the sight of a gigantic snake that had lowered itself unawares to him.

An even more horrible snake has lowered himself on the earth, seeking to devour God's people. Your escape depends on how well you are willing to listen, evaluate and then act. Being conscious of the devourer, David wrote, "Your laws are my treasure; they are my heart's delight. (Psalm 119:111NLT).

God has left his word for us to order our steps.

Pray with me: "*Lord help me to continually listen to you and behave accordingly. Amen*"

In your difficult times, what God needs is perfect obedience. Your challenges are not room to dishonour God. Irrespective of the crisis, God desires “Shema Levot”, ‘a hearing heart.’ A hearing heart is one that is intent on, committed to, and devoted to executing God’s word whether or not it is convenient. If an earthly, imperfect, and dispensable father can give instruction to his son to evade the snake, how much more our loving father? His laws are good and just.

If you fully obey the Lord your God and carefully keep all his commands that I am giving you today, the Lord your God will set you high above all the nations of the world. You will experience all these blessings if you obey the Lord your God (Deuteronomy 28:1-2 NLT)

God does not need merely ‘follow-ship’, he needs obedience. Purpose in your heart to obey God in all seasons.

May you, as you navigate the difficult terrain of life, understand that God requires total, undiluted obedience; that is the best way.

Chapter 11

Open Access

"At that moment, the curtain in the sanctuary of the Temple was torn in two, from top to bottom. The earth shook, rocks split apart," (Matthew 27: 51NLT)

The veil was the only thing separating the Holy Place from the Holy of Holies. A closer observation would reveal the Holy Place to be the that assigned to man and the Holy of Holies the place reserved for God. In essence, the veil is a vivid partition between man and God symbolizing the barrier between sinful humanity and an absolute God. A thrilling scene unfolds: the veil was torn from top to bottom, ruling out any suspicion of foul play and creating an opening wide enough for the vilest sinner to have access to God.

Lift your hands and declare: "Lord thank you for renting the veil and granting access to your kingdom. I did not earn it, neither did I deserve it, Thank for open access."

My practice as educator sometimes requires me to distinguish between proprietary and open software. Proprietary software is a program for which the owner, developer, or publisher retains the intellectual property rights and therefore is not free to be used by all. Prior to Jesus' redemptive plan, relationship with God was like a proprietary software: it was not available to all.

Access to the Most Holy Place was reserved to the high priest and so costly that his entry there was limited. To use proprietary software, one must apply to the publisher, who is sometimes separate from the owner.

As with this closed software, a person desiring pardon for their sins had to apply to the priest and provide the satisfactory honorarium. If one is unable to access the publisher of a no-free software or is incapable of paying the fees, the desired need would go unsatisfied. Can you imagine the price of a turtle dove or a bull in this era where there is an even greater disparity between the haves and the have nots? Depending on where you live, some proprietary items may be inaccessible.

A relationship with God was strictly available to Jews, ruling out Gentile nations. Failing to adhere to the rules governing intellectual property rights could result in a fine or even imprisonment. As with this software, any attempt to violate any of the laws could result in instant death. There was no room for mercy; you were either right or wrong. Jesus in his sovereignty saw this type of relationship as being too rigid, lacking the harmony of peace, joy, and love. And so, He came up with a better plan mimicking the open source software. An open source software is one in which the copyright bearer gives permission to all to use freely. Jesus, by paying the full price of the proprietary, now makes it available to all.

“He came to his own people, and even they rejected him. But to all who believed him and accepted him, he gave the right to become children of God.” (John 1: 11-12 NLT)

He became that one lamb, making remission possible for all, despite gender, nationality, race, socioeconomic status or educational background. He tore the veil allowing all to access a relationship with God. He discontinued the legalistic process of prayer through an intermediary by promoting us all to priests.

“He has made us a Kingdom of priests for God his Father. All glory and power to him forever and ever! Amen.” (Rev 1: 6NLT)

Jesus declared our bodies the temple of the Lord, the habitat of the Holy Spirit from which worship should rise.

“And don’t you realize that if a man joins himself to a prostitute, he becomes one body with her? For the Scriptures say, ‘The two are united into one.’”1 (Corinthians 6: 16 NLT)

Lift your hands and thank God for the open access awarded to us.

One of the provisions made available through God’s Open Access plan was the promotion to priest, permitting us to pray directly to God about our sins, weaknesses, fears, doubts, and anything else as we deem necessary. Prayer is a honest conversation with God to adore, confess, thank, or make requests. God only responds to our earnest, honest, and sincere request.

"The earnest prayer of a righteous person has great power and produces wonderful results." (James 5:16NLT)

Some years ago, I was at the point of giving up on God. Things were just spiraling out of control and I thought God was not hearing me. Have you ever been in a situation where you just think God has gone deaf? I want to declare that prayer still works, and God is still responding to prayer.

"And we are confident that he hears us whenever we ask for anything that pleases him." (1 John 5: 14NLT).

I was an evangelist preaching across the length and breadth of Jamaica but struggling to access necessities. It got so bad that I could not afford soap for laundry. The already limited clothes were piling up in a corner, and clean outfits were becoming scarce. The straw that broke the camel's back was God's silence concerning my little favour, the desire to pursue tertiary education. It was August and I needed a change, one that was just not happening quick enough. How do you continue praying when the signs of hope become dim? This requires senseless, relentless pursuit of God. Job declared in the midst of terror, "Though he slay me yet will I trust him." [Job 13:15] Situations sometimes get worse before they get better. Storms appear to test your stability. Can you still pray when it seems like God is ignoring you? Take Job for instance: he lost his wealth, his children, and his health. To make matters worse, he was accused of sinning and was encouraged to curse God and die. It is unwise to halt prayer expecting God to respond. Pursue God relentlessly.

Pray with me: *"Lord help me to be faithful in praying when it seems you are not hearing me. Amen."*

One Sunday afternoon I hustled home, a place I had to climb through a window to access. When I looked at the little table where I stored my tinned mackerel, the emptiness was more obvious than a stop sign. It was as if God was socially distancing and favour was quarantined in a far-off inaccessible, fortified city. The presence of difficulties, lack, and shortages is evidence that you need to make your faith plea. May the thing that bothers you most move you to unremitting prayer.

"O God listen to my cry! Hear my prayer! From the ends of the earth, I cry to you for help when my heart is overwhelmed. Lead me to the towering rock of safety," (Psalm 61:1-2NLT)

Prayer is translated from the Hebrew word 'tephillah' which means 'to beg' while perceiving yourself as an inferior, dependent being, pleading to a superior, supreme and independent God. All that I want is in Him.

Declare this with me: "All I need is in God; nothing missing, nothing lacking".

That afternoon, I engaged God in a conversation, outlining in detail my desires, and how I honestly felt. I remember stating, "Even if you must send the help from England, allow it to happen." The pureness of your prayer will attract the attention of God. Prayer is more about expressing your sincere need and how you feel than it is about your tone, eloquence, and sound.

"In those days when you pray, I will listen." (Jeremiah 29:12NLT)

God values our conversation and always delights in one-to-one talk. Do not expect if you do not ask. That very day, my neighbour brought me some groceries and, as if that were not enough, the following morning, I heard a call coming from the front of the residence. A young lady appeared and said, "Pastor, God told me to do your laundry." My clothes were washed, dried, folded and returned to me that afternoon. One week after, a lady attended church and gifted the first financial aid to my tertiary education. What baffled my mind was when she said, "Last week Sunday, I was home praying and the Lord said, 'Nicholas from Jamaica needs help to pay tuition.'" At the time I knew no one from that address neither did I have any earthly medium to make such contact. If God can send a total stranger to my little community to help me understand that He hears and responds to sincere prayers, what will He not do for you? I am further mystified by the fact that this lady did not wire, or mail the funds, but brought it herself. God enjoys supplying the needs of His children. A personal delivery reinforces the love and faithfulness of God.

Open access has been approved, you can go in and speak with the king.

Elijah was as human as we are, and yet when he prayed earnestly that no rain would fall, none fell for three and a half years! (James 5:17 NLT)

The outcome is tied to your prayer so stay in tune with God. As Elijah extended his effectiveness in prayer to the weather, expand your prayers when it is hardest.

In your difficult times, use prayer as a reliable technique. Open access is yours, pray more.

As you navigate through difficult times, may you revel in the open access to the throne of God.

Chapter 12

Triumph Over the Monster

For God has not given us a spirit of fear and timidity, but of power, love, and self-discipline. (2 Timothy 1: 7NLT)

Perhaps one of the most crucial steps in navigating difficult times is the discarding of fear from the outset. Paul, having noticed the obvious reticent attitude of his mentee, challenged him to vanquish fear immediately. Fear is like a virus that not only affects one psychologically and spiritually, but physically as well. It is perhaps the most dangerous infection for any believer to be afflicted with.

Pray with me: *"Lord help to detect any spirit operating illegally in my domain. Relieve me of any such effects of fear in Jesus' name amen".*

A snake revealed is not as effective as a snake hidden. If we are to conquer fear, we must recognize its traits and signs. Sometimes, we are unable to identify our fears and the impact they are having on us. In this passage, it was the discerning eye of an alert mentor that made the diagnosis. May the Lord appoint destiny helpers that are able to detect the stronghold of the enemy.

I declare that the habitat for fear will be identified in the name of Jesus.

The vigilant mentor not only detected the fear but sought to determine its source. A tree that is cut at the stem has a greater chance to spring again to even greater dimension than one that is amputated at the root. Paul reinforces the dogma that God is not the source of one's fear. Sometimes, we can recognize fear but are incapable of locating the source. Making it absolutely clear that the fear is not of God is cementing the fact it is of the devil; misdiagnosis is even more dangerous than no diagnosis. It is not enough to know what is wrong but be ignorant of the root cause. Paul's role in this scripture reinforces the idea that there are no lone soldiers in God's army. Every Timothy needs a Paul to watch over, guide, remind, and empower to conquer, while all 'Pauls' need 'a Timothy' to minister to, to guide, and to fulfill one's purpose. It also projects the maturity that Paul must possess to help Timothy overcome.

May God align you in this season with the right people to help you to conquer all attacks sent by the enemy.

From time to time we all face situations that make us fearful. For some people it is the fear of confrontation, for others it is the fear to socialize with a new audience, while for others, it is the fear of the unknown. Some are worried about the uncertainties in life.

What are you fearful of?

Pray with me*: "Lord reveal to me the things that I am fearful of today. Help me to conquer fear.*

Studies show that fear weakens the immune system which is the 'military base' of the human body, warding off external attacks called diseases. A dilapidated defence system will give rise to diseases in the human body. Fear also reduces fertility, advances aging and causes premature death. The enemy's intention is to destroy you.

The thief's purpose is to steal and kill and destroy. (St John 10:10NLT)

I declare that fear will not be your portion; your immune system will not be destroyed at the expense of fear; you will be fruitful and multiply as needed, and you will not age or die prematurely because of fear.

Anything that is noticed in the physical is parallel to the spiritual. The devil seeks to not only destroy you in the physical realm but also in the spiritual realm. Fear can have greater consequence in the spiritual than the physical. It is clear then that God is not the giver of fear.

Declare with me: "I serve notice to every instrument of fear occupying my residence. My body is the temple of the Holy Spirit. The only spirit that will reign in or over me is the Holy Spirit."

The fear virus often unknowingly attaches itself to the believer. To combat fear, the believer must acquire an antivirus powerful enough to rid them of the enemy's trap. The Bible makes the following recommendation: Put on:

- ℟ The helmet of Salvation. Salvation plays a key role in dismantling the source of fear.

Have you accepted Christ as your Lord and saviour?

....

....

- ℟ The Breastplate of Righteousness. It is righteousness that will provide the protection needed for vital organs such as the heart.

I declare you will never cry over that thing sprouting fear and doubt. You are delivered instantly in Jesus name.

℟ The Belt of Truth. Honesty is critical. Make a list of all the things that you are fearful about and, along with a trusted friend, pray for deliverance from them.

Things I am Fearful About
1)
2)
3)
4)
5)
6)
7)
8)
9)
10)
11)
12)

℞ The Shoes of Peace. Sometimes the trouble we create is what fuels our fears. Write a reflection on the last 3 days. Was there anything that you did that contributed to your fear? Apologize, ask for forgiveness and desist from doing it again.

My Reflection

- The Shield of Faith. The interlocking shield of faith is not only used for defence but for attack; attack your fears with the Word. Make a list of 10 promises from the Bible and declare them over your life daily.

Promises
1)
2)
3)
4)
5)
6)
7)
8)
9)
10)

USE….

- The Sword of the Spirit (The Word). The sword was the most lethal weapon in the Roman Empire. I want to declare that the words in your mouth are more dangerous than anything in the enemy's toolbox. Make small charts with verses of scripture and post them around your house, office, and cars. Declare them every time the fear comes knocking.

Take a picture and attach in the space below

Paste Picture Here

AND…….

℞ Prayer: This is an honest conversation with God. Make a daily appointment to talk with God about your fears.

MY PRAYER PLAN

Starting Date……………

Time………………………

May you, as you navigate life's difficult pathways as a believer, enlist the power of the Lord to identify and defeat fear.

Let us Pray: "*I declare that my fears are defeated. I am released from every psychological prison. I declare I am free to fulfil my purpose. I declare fear is conquered in Jesus' name.*

CONCLUSION

Hardship is inevitable as we go through life; one has to decide how he is going to deal with these crises. Is the decision to throw your hands up in the air and give up an option? Maybe that is what some people have done. Even though that is a suggestion, it is neither a logical nor a spiritual one. God desires us to exercise child-like dependence on Him and if we choose a different path, we will find ourselves in a big rut.

As you have read through the pages of "Positive Vibrations, Navigating Difficult Times", I trust that they will inspire you to reject the stretcher and pull your way through. Throughout your wilderness experiences, listen to God's voice as there are lessons to be learned and you will have a different mindset.

Tell yourself that you will not diminish if God is leading you. In putting on the whole armour of God - prayer, the word of God, a mind fortified by assurances of salvation and an inclination to the way of peace, be assured that you will have the victory; the Lord goes before you and fights all your battles. You only need to stand still and behold His salvation.

Trust the Lord in the experiences along the journey of your life, no matter how manageable or difficult they are. As you give God what He requires, you can be guaranteed that He will not let you down. If your close friends and family care so much about you, imagine what God can do on your behalf. An intimate relationship with God is the best thing that could ever happen to you. He has offered open access to His throne and is never busy. Call on His name; He likes to hear His children's worship and delights in being there for them.

You can step forth on the rest of your journey with confidence, knowing that, the same God who has provided all the resources on which countless believers have relied for sustenance, support and eventual victory will be faithful to you.

How To Navigate Through Difficult Times?

Navigating difficult times will require you to:

- ℞ Pray to God (See James 5:16)
- ℞ Trust God (See Psalms 118:8)
- ℞ Obey God (See Deuteronomy 28:1)
- ℞ Listen to God (See Luke 11:28)
- ℞ Hope in God (See Psalms 42:5)
- ℞ Know your worth (See Jeremiah 29:11)
- ℞ Give God what He Requires (See John 14:15-21)
- ℞ Use the name (See Psalms 34:6)
- ℞ Know whose you are (See Isaiah 43:1-2)
- ℞ Pursue God relentlessly

BLESSING

May the LORD bless you

and protect you.

May the LORD smile on you

and be gracious to you.

May the LORD show you his favor

and give you his peace.'

May you allow Holy Spirit to occupy you

And influence you and promote Christ

May life be transformed as you apply the principles written in this book.

God Bless You

Notes

Notes

Notes

Notes

Printed by Amazon Italia Logistica S.r.l.
Torrazza Piemonte (TO), Italy

53969973R00067